D0466263

A History of Germs

THE BLACK DEATH

By Jim Ollhoff

VISIT US AT
WWW.ABDOPUBLISHING.COM

Printed in the United States.

PRINTED ON RECYCLED PAPER

Editor: John Hamilton
Graphic Design: Sue Hamilton
Cover Design: John Hamilton
Cover Photo: Photo Researchers
Interior Photos and Illustrations: Alamy-pgs 17 & 29; CDC-pg 16; Corbis-pgs 6, 9, 19 &, 20; Getty Images-pgs 7 & 18; The Granger Collection-pgs 4, 11, 15, & 27; iStockphoto-pgs 3, 4, 5, & 21; Jupiterimages-pgs 13, 22, 25, 26, & 31; North Wind Picture Archives-pg 28; and Photo Researchers-1, 8, 10, 12, 23, 24, & 25.

Library of Congress Cataloging-in-Publication Data

Ollhoff, Jim, 1959-
  The black death / Jim Ollhoff.
      p. cm. – (A history of germs)
  Includes index.
  ISBN 978-1-60453-497-9
  1. Plague–Juvenile literature. I. Title.

  QR201.P5O45 2010
  616.9'232–dc22

                          2008055061

CONTENTS

THE BLACK DEATH

It was the end of the world. During the years 1347 to 1350, a mysterious plague swept through Europe. People died by the hundreds, then the thousands. Then, by the millions. When victims got sick, they developed massive swellings that turned purple and black. Too weak to get out of bed, they began to vomit blood. Within a few days, they were dead.

The plague became known as the Black Death. Before this great tragedy, Europe had been secure with its mighty feudal kingdoms. Cities had thick walls to protect people from invaders. Giant cathedrals reached to the sky. Universities were beginning, promising the hope of education. People felt safe and secure.

Artwork from 1349 shows many people bringing plague victims to be buried.

One out of every three people who contracted the Black Death died.

Then, the plague struck. Before it was over, 25 to 40 million people died in Europe alone. One out of every three people who contracted the disease died. In some cities, more than half of the people died. In other towns, there was no one left to bury the dead. Burials were so quick and shallow that wild animals sometimes dug up the corpses. In some towns, relatives had to carry dead family members out of their homes and stack them on carts, so the bodies could be hauled away and buried in mass graves. People wondered if everyone in the world was going to die.

People today called the plague "the Black Death" because of the blackened skin of those who were infected. But in the years that the disease was active, it was called "the Great Mortality," or simply, "the end of the world."

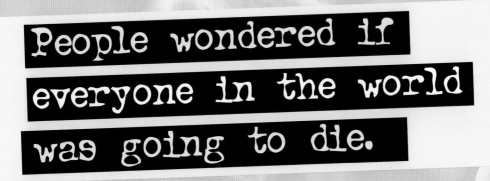

People wondered if everyone in the world was going to die.

In 1347, the bubonic plague entered Europe through the cities of Constantinople (today's Istanbul, Turkey), Genoa (in modern-day northern Italy), and the island of Sicily. Infected people came by boat, and then accidentally gave the plague to people who were in the cities. The plague spread throughout the cities. When people left the cities, the plague went with them. Like a deadly hitchhiker, the plague followed the normal trading and traveling routes.

By December 1348, the plague had reached northern Europe. By June of 1349, northern England was infected. The plague reached Norway in May 1349. Legend says that an English boat drifted into a harbor in Norway. Everyone in the boat was dead, except for one man, who then infected the people of Norway.

The bubonic plague probably entered Europe through Italy. Over the next two years, it quickly spread through England and up into Norway.

From 1347-1349, it's estimated that 25-40 million people died in Europe.

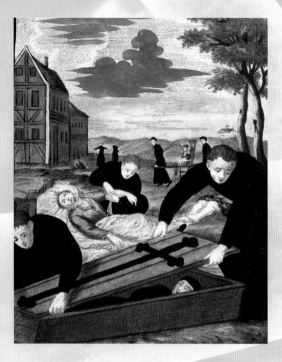

The plague hit cities hard, because people lived closer together and there was a greater chance of getting infected. Many cities lost half their population. Some areas, such as eastern England and cities in Italy, lost 60 percent of their population. In Florence, Italy, almost 70 percent of the citizens died. In the span of three years, somewhere between 25 million and 40 million people died in Europe.

Religious leaders, medical doctors, and anyone who tended the sick often died of the plague themselves.

Some historians say that a fourth of the population of Europe was lost. Others say half of the population fell to the plague. The best estimates say that about a third of the population died.

Perhaps 75 million people died worldwide. By 1352, the plague was in Moscow. It had spread to North Africa and the Middle East as well.

Some professions suffered more than others. Doctors and clergy suffered the most, since they tended to the sick. In Montpellier, France, there was a monastery with 140 monks. Only seven of them survived.

The psychological terror was almost as terrible as the physical toll of the plague. People of that time did not understand bacteria or disease transmission. They did not know what was causing the deaths. They never knew whom it would strike next. They felt helpless because they did not know how to stop it. Many people believed that God was punishing them. This made the misery even more difficult, because they then asked themselves, "What did we do to deserve this?"

In Florence, Italy, almost 70 percent of the city's population died during the plague years. People wondered why this was happening to them.

WHAT CAUSED THE PLAGUE?

The cause of the Black Plague wasn't discovered until 1899. It was a bacterium called *Yersinia pestis*. It lived in the digestive system of fleas. The fleas lived on rats. When the rats died, the fleas went looking for more food. When the fleas bit people, the bacteria were injected into their bloodstream. Then, victims infected others by coughing near them, or even breathing.

There were actually three different types of the plague, even though they are often lumped together and called "the bubonic plague."

An image of the plague bacteria *Yersinia pestis*. This bacteria causes bubonic plague.

A 14th-century image of a physician lancing a plague-caused bubo. These blackened swellings appeared on the neck, armpits, and other areas.

The bubonic plague was the most common, and the most survivable, of the three types. About 30 percent of those who got the bubonic type died. The bubonic plague was named after a symptom called buboes, which were blackened swellings on the neck, armpits, and other areas.

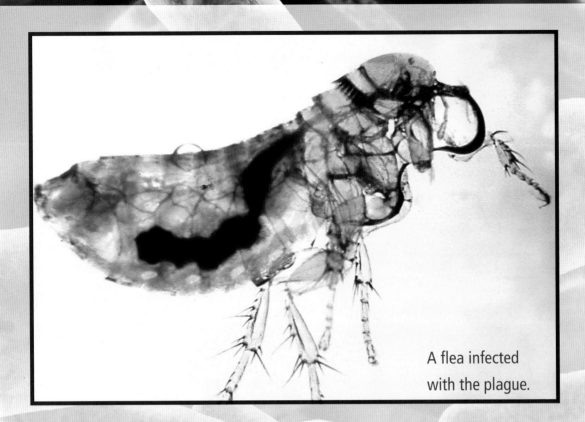

A flea infected
with the plague.

The second type was called pneumonic plague. It infected the lungs, and was very contagious when victims coughed.

The third type was called septicemic plague. Septicemia is when blood is poisoned by bacteria or toxins they produce. Septicemic plague was less common, but almost always fatal.

There were a number of other factors that made people more susceptible to the plague. There was a small climate change in the early 1300s. This caused more droughts and floods. Farm crops didn't grow as well. The resulting shortage of food left many people malnourished. When people are malnourished, they are more susceptible to disease.

Further, the shortage of food may have forced rats to move closer to humans, where there is more food. Since the rats were carrying the fleas with the plague, more people got sick.

Another factor was that cities were growing rapidly. This meant more people had to eat. So, there were more slaughterhouses, where cattle and other animals were butchered for their meat. Large amounts of animal entrails were left lying around. This attracted rats, bringing them closer to humans.

With the growth of the cities came an increase in human waste. There were no sewers or flush toilets. Many communities' only law about human sewage was to shout, "Look out below!" before throwing a pot of human sewage into the streets. This also attracted rats, and thus made humans closer to the fleas that lived on the rats.

In rural areas, many homes were made out of thatch and mud bricks. Farm animals often lived in the same house as the people. This made easy access for rats and fleas. Bathing was uncommon, which meant lots of dirt, fleas, and lice.

Black Rat

During the plague years, ships coming into harbors were often quarantined for 40 days. This meant that no one was allowed to leave the ship in order to prevent sick people from bringing disease into the port city. People knew that the disease spread from person to person, so the quarantines might have worked a little. But rats could easily make it to shore on the ropes that moored the ships. Since the rats spread the disease, even just having a ship docked nearby could mean infection in the city.

Plague-ridden fleas jumped from rats to people.

HOW DID THE PLAGUE START?

Scientists don't know for sure when rats became the carriers of the Black Death. But they think the bacteria first became deadly in northeast China. Over time, bacteria go through changes called mutations, which can make them more dangerous. This deadly mutation may have hit human populations in Asia in the early 1320s.

Chinese writers in the 1330s wrote about a terrible disease. Although firm evidence is sketchy, it may have killed a third of the Chinese population at the time. Historians can look back and trace a series of local epidemics in northeast China, and then to towns farther to the west. As traders or warring armies moved west, the disease went with them. The fleas and rats traveled in the supplies. And with raiding armies on horseback, the disease traveled very fast.

Historians have discovered evidence of plague epidemics in the Gobi Desert and Mongolia in the early 1330s. The plague moved west to what is today Kyrgyzstan. In 1346, the plague reached the shores of the Caspian Sea. Finally, it reached the doors of Europe.

On the north side of the Black Sea, there was a trading settlement named Caffa. The post was operated by traders from Genoa, Italy. But in 1346, a Mongol army laid siege to Caffa, hoping to drive them out. However, the Mongol soldiers began dying from a mysterious disease at an alarming rate.

In 1346, a Mongol army attacked Caffa, a trading settlement on the north side of the Black Sea. However, the Mongol soldiers began dying from a mysterious disease.

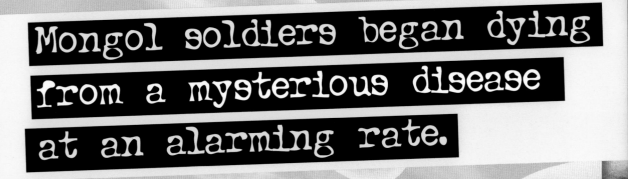

Mongol soldiers began dying from a mysterious disease at an alarming rate.

There's a bizarre story, which was written years after the siege, that explains how the Italian traders of Caffa got the plague. The story says that the Mongol leader put the bodies of his dead soldiers into catapults and launched them into the city, with the hope of infecting the inhabitants.

Many historians don't believe the catapulting story. The rats carrying the disease lived around the Mongol army. It's probably more likely that the rats got into the city through small openings and cracks in the wall. But whether the story is true or not, the people of Caffa got the plague.

The Mongol army, their numbers decimated by disease, finally left the siege of Caffa. By early 1347, the Genoan traders returned home, and they brought the Black Death with them.

Boats from Caffa arrived in Genoa, Constantinople, Sicily, and other ports. Stories say that some ships ran aground, with no one left alive on the ships. Rats escaped to the land. Looters stole cargo from the ships, which also spread the disease.

Disease-carrying sailors from Caffa were probably not alone in spreading the Black Death. The plague also likely spread overland as people migrated from country to country. But, by the spring of 1347, the Black Death was hitting major cities, and hitting them hard.

Actual size

An enlargement of a blood-engorged flea and, by comparison, its actual size. These tiny creatures killed millions of people through the centuries.

Death takes the lives of a merchant and a sailor.

WHAT WAS IT LIKE TO GET THE PLAGUE?

The Black Death was a painful, horrible disease to catch, and it spread in a horrifying way. Rats carried fleas. Fleas carried inside them the bacteria that caused the plague. When they bit people, some of the bacteria got into the bloodstream. The rats eventually died, and the fleas died, too.

When a person got infected, either through a fleabite or from another infected person, their infection began to spread. The infection would spread to the lymph nodes in the neck, armpits, and groin. A high fever would take over the body, and their arms and legs would start to ache. They would be in bed by this time.

The infection spread through the body.

The lymph nodes began to swell, sometimes into huge baseball-sized tumors. These swellings, called buboes, turned dark purple or black, filling with infected fluid. Sometimes the swellings would burst. The person began heavy, labored breathing, and then they would start vomiting blood. From the first onset of plague symptoms, death could occur one to four days later.

About 70 percent of those who got infected ended up dying a horrible death. Some people survived the disease, and some lucky souls were naturally immune to the infection.

Is the Bubonic Plague still around today?

Yes, the bubonic plague still exists today. In the United States, it is often found in mountain or desert areas. But today, we have a weapon that the people in the 1300s did not have: antibiotics. In the early 1900s, scientists began to develop medicines called antibiotics, such as penicillin, that kill bacteria. Powerful, modern antibiotics today usually kill the bubonic plague bacteria. Also, insecticides effectively kill the fleas that can spread the disease.

A biologist in Bombay, India, brushes a dead rat for fleas. Today, modern science and powerful medicines are used to find and kill the bubonic plague bacteria before it can harm people.

DESPERATE CURES

In the 1300s, doctors had little knowledge of disease. They did not have microscopes, so they couldn't see bacteria. They were completely baffled by the Black Death and how it spread. They were desperate to do something—anything—to help the suffering people.

Many doctors thought the disease had come from an earthquake that released putrid underground air. The foul air must have caused the disease, they said. To combat the plague, people were instructed to spend time in their gardens smelling flowers and clean air.

Doctors desperately wanted to keep their patients from dying of the plague. But, without knowing what caused the disease, none of their ideas worked.

Some people thought the disease came from a comet. Some doctors said it was a result of being sad, so they instructed people to think happy thoughts and listen to good music. Other "cures" included not sleeping too much, not doing too much exercise, not eating fish, using more perfume, or burning special kinds of wood. Some thought that a hot onion, applied to a bubo, would draw

Leeches were used to drain plague victims' blood. This only weakened the already very sick patient.

out the poison. Of course, none of these remedies had any effect on the devastating disease.

Some doctors said the illness happened because people had too much blood. They applied leeches to drain the excess blood. Ironically, this hastened the death of the infected person. Other authorities said bathing spread the disease, so they instructed people not to take baths. Again, this probably made them more susceptible to fleas, and thus more likely to contract the disease.

In plague-stricken London, authorities locked the city walls, hoping to keep out the Black Death. Half of the population died.

Flagellants went from town to town, whipping themselves. They believed if they punished themselves, God would spare people from the plague.

Since people didn't understand science in the 1300s, many blamed God. They thought God was punishing them. They didn't know why God would punish them, but what other reason could there be?

It was during this time that people known as flagellants emerged. *Flagellant* is from a Latin word meaning "whip." Flagellants believed that if they punished themselves, God would spare people from the plague. They went from town to town, whipping themselves in the hope of earning the favor of God. Some even whipped themselves to death. The flagellants also became very hateful toward Jewish people, because it was the Jews who crucified Jesus Christ. The flagellants believed that God was punishing them for letting Jews live in the area, and so they harassed and even killed Jews. In October 1349, the Pope condemned the flagellants and ordered authorities to imprison them.

Some doctors, knowing they were at risk because they worked near infected plague victims, designed protective suits. They wore a layer of thick cloth, which hung down to the floor. They also wore a mask, with a large pouch on the face. The mask looked like a giant bird beak. The pouch was full of herbs and flowers to protect against the putrid smell they thought caused the disease. They also put

A plague doctor's protective suit.

red eyepieces in the mask. They thought this would protect them in case simply seeing a sick person caused the disease.

Doctors wore protective suits to keep from getting the plague.

WHAT STOPPED THE PLAGUE?

After years of horror, the Black Death finally stopped, but not because of any cures devised by the people. At the end of the year 1350, and the beginning of 1351, the plague simply ceased. Its final toll was devastating. It had cut like a knife through Europe for three years, killing between 25 and 40 million people.

The plague would hit certain areas over the next 400 years, but it was always a local epidemic. It never again had the deadly force it did before. It hit London in 1665, Marseilles, France, in 1720, and Moscow in 1771, but was never as deadly or contagious as it was in the 1300s.

From 1720-1722, the plague killed about 100,000 people in and around the area of Marseilles, France.

Changes in society made the plague less infectious. There were fewer people after the plague, and that meant less crowding, so there was less chance of sharing the disease. Better nutrition may have helped people stave off the plague. People began to bathe more, and wear higher-quality clothes, which meant fewer fleas. The shipping industry became better at quarantining ships that came from diseased areas.

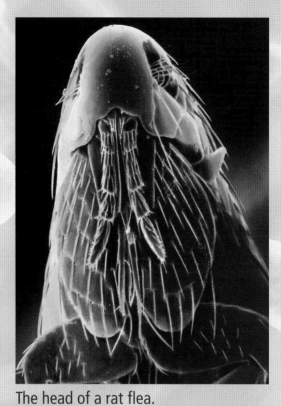

The head of a rat flea.

People began to build better houses. In many places tiles began to replace thatched roofs, which made homes safer from fire. It also made it less likely that fleas would drop in from the roof.

Perhaps the biggest reason for the plague's demise was that it ran out of fuel—it simply ran out of people to kill. Some people survived the plague, and so developed a better immunity to the disease. It's also possible that the plague bacteria mutated into a less deadly form.

Perhaps the reason the plague stopped was that it ran out of people to kill.

THE LEGACY OF THE BLACK DEATH

The Black Death was gone, but it left behind a very different world. It changed the future of Europe.

As the plague began to wane, it left behind many problems, aside from grief and suffering. One-third of the workers were gone. This left a chronic shortage of people to do the farming, run the mills, and help manufacture materials. The shortage caused a slump in construction and trade. Wars were scaled down or stopped altogether. With the drastic shortage of workers, there was less farming, which caused food shortages.

Before the Black Death, workers called serfs sometimes worked for little or no pay. But with fewer workers available, they became very valuable. They demanded better pay. If landowners wouldn't pay higher wages, workers could walk to the next town—or even the next farm—and get a better-paying job. Serfs could even walk off the job and find cheap land for sale, becoming farmers themselves.

The plague also caused an oversupply of products, because there were fewer people to purchase goods. So, prices went down even as wages increased. This was good for the average worker.

After the plague, serfs demanded, and often got, better pay for their work.

On the other hand, landowners saw their wealth evaporate because of high labor costs and lower food prices. The rich became poorer and the poor became richer.

Financial businesses were terribly disrupted. People who lent money often had no one to collect from, since whole families had been wiped out. Many people who owed money had no one to pay it back to, since many creditors also died.

As cities got back on their feet, they created better sanitation, burial practices, and hospitals. Medical schools emphasized the physical sciences. This helped prepare society for the scientific method— proposing a theory and testing it by observable facts.

There was some anger and resentment at the church's inability to stop the plague. This set the stage for the Reformation, where many abuses and superstitions were largely swept out of the church.

The legacy of the Black Death is perhaps best portrayed in art. Paintings show horrific scenes of the dead and dying, with worms and demons eating people's flesh. Many paintings show skeletons living with people in daily scenes. Skeletons stand next to people in scenes of hunting or eating. Peasants dance with skeletons at festivals.

Today, the paintings seem shocking. But they remind us that even in the midst of horror, loss, and death, life goes on.

People fleeing from the plague are surrounded by skeletons (death).

Ring around the rosy, a pocket full of posies. Ashes, Ashes, we all fall down.

Some historians suggest this popular children's song came from the 1800s. But other historians believe this song came from the time of the Black Death. The rosy was the bubo swelling, and the ring was the circular infection around it. "Pocket full of posies" refers to the practice of carrying flowers around in pockets, as protection from the bad air. "Ashes, ashes" referred to the burning of the dead, and "we all fall down" refers to the death of almost everyone.

GLOSSARY

ANTIBIOTICS

A group of medicines that kill harmful bacteria. These medicines were created in the early 1900s.

BUBO

A large swelling that is characteristic of those with bubonic plague.

FLAGELLANTS

Extreme religious fanatics who believed God would stop the plague if they punished themselves.

PNEUMONIC PLAGUE

A type of plague that infects the lungs.

QUARANTINE

The practice of keeping infected people separate, so they won't infect healthy people.

SEPTICEMIC PLAGUE

A type of plague that infected the blood, and was very lethal.

THATCH

Dry vegetation, such as reeds and straw. Thatch was often used to make roofs.

YERSINIA PESTIS

The bacteria responsible for the bubonic plague.

The Plague Pit.

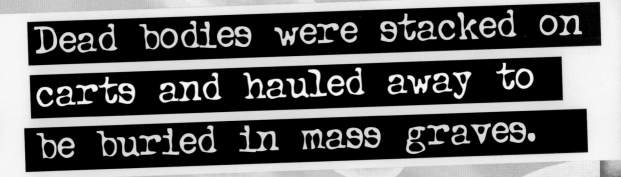

Dead bodies were stacked on carts and hauled away to be buried in mass graves.

INDEX